I am

Shonda Miles

Copyright

Copyright © 2016 Shonda Miles

To My Sweet

Jasmine

You are my favorite

girl in the world

I am beautiful.

I am smart.

I am happy.

I am loved.

I am kind.

I am perfect just the way I am.

I am strong.

I am helpful.

I choose my attitude.

I am positive.

I believe in myself.

I am a winner.

I love to learn.

I am blessed.

I never give up.

I work hard.

I am loved.

I am healthy.

I am extraordinary.

I like myself.

I am pretty.

I can do anything I put my
mind to.

I love myself.

I am talented and gifted.

I am special.

I make friends easily.

I am generous.

My family and friends
love me for who I am.

I am important.

I am happy.

I am awesome.

Black Child poem by Useni Eugene Perkins'

Hey Black Child

Do you know who you are
Who you really are
Do you know you can be
What you want to be
If you try to be
What you can be

Hey Black Child
Do you know where you are going
Where you're really going
Do you know you can learn
What you want to learn
If you try to learn
What you can learn

Hey Black Child
Do you know you are strong
I mean really strong
Do you know you can do
What you want to do
If you try to do
What you can do

Hey Black Child
Be what you can be
Learn what you must learn

Do what you can do
And tomorrow your nation
Will be what you what it to be

Before You Leave

I need your help. When you go to the next page, Kindle gives you an opportunity to share your thoughts and opinions through your Facebook and Twitter account. If you believe your friends and family will benefit from this book, please share your thoughts with them. You might change someone's life, and I would be eternally grateful to you.

If you feel strongly about the contributions this book made to your life, please take a few seconds to post a 5-star review on Amazon. Very few people ever leave 5-star review. So it is a big deal if you do. Writing a 5-star review is like tipping me $25. I really appreciate the gesture. I feel like a million bucks whenever I get a glowing review.

If you have any questions, you can reach me via Shondamiles@yahoo.com. I will try to respond to your questions as soon as possible. You can also connect with me on Facebook and Twitter.

Journal

Journal

Journal

Journal

Journal

Journal

Journal

Journal

Journal

Journal

Other books by Author

10 Ways to Write an EBook every 10 days

101 Success Questions that will change your life

Remote Medical Coding Jobs

Tips for Staring an Online Business

How to Love Your Spouse again

How to Double Your Income in 12 Months or less

50 Tips to Jumpstart Your Success

50 Streams of Income

How to Get the Job You Want

21 Ways to Start a Marriage off Right

18 Ways to Break into Coding

21 Ways to make a Blended Family Work

I am

Marty learns to swim

30 days to being a better Christian

How to create an audio product

About the Author

Shonda Miles has been self-employed for 18 years. She has owned businesses ranging from an online retail store to a Training Company.

Shonda Miles is the CEO of Shonda Miles International, a company helping organizations and individuals improve performance and achieve their goals. Shonda Miles is here to help you achieve your full potential. Her purpose is to help millions of people achieve their goals and live their God given talent.

Shonda Miles is an Author, Entrepreneur, Speaker, Personal Development Trainer, Business Consultant and Business Coach. She loves reading Nonfiction books, writing business books and shopping. Personal Development is her mission. Shonda speaks, blogs and writes about a variety of personal development topics such as Time Management, Success, Goal Setting and having a Positive Attitude.

Shonda's goal is to help others achieve the level of success they desire.

Shonda Miles is a MBA Graduate. She has several successful businesses.

Shonda Miles can be reached at info@shondamiles.com or via her website at www.shondamiles.com.

Made in the USA
San Bernardino, CA
14 February 2019